This book belongs to:

JASON

Mokey Fraggle's New Colors

by Emily Paul   illustrated by Larry Di Fiori

Muppet Press

My name is Mokey Fraggle,
  and my paints are fresh and new.
And I'd like to paint a picture
  that is especially for you.

I've got each color that I need.
  The problem is to choose
The things that I should paint for you.
  What subjects should I use?

With RED, I could paint radishes and juicy apples, too,
Or some roses in the garden, if I went and picked a few.
I could paint some red galoshes, an umbrella, or I might
Paint my best friend Red's red sweater,
    which she wears both day and night.

With BLUE, I could paint bluebirds
or a lovely summer sky,
Or the berries Boober gathers up to bake into a pie.
Or his apron or his basket or his scarf or silly hat,
Or his very favorite cookbook. Hmm.
Now, maybe I'll paint that!

Now, what to use my YELLOW for?
Some daffodils? The sun?
Or some lemons in the garden?
Do you think that would be fun?

And while I'm in the garden,
I could use the color GREEN
To paint the greatest grass and leaves
that you have ever seen!

My ORANGE will paint oranges
or carrots, it is true...
But if oranges won't work,
I guess that Gobo's hat will do.

Now PURPLE could be lilacs
or some plums upon the shelf.
And I guess it's even possible
that I could paint myself.

But wait! I've got a great idea!
Why did I make a fuss?
If I want to use my colors,
then I'll just paint all of us!